Fairy Nurse Rhia

Why the Starlings Dance

A Violet & Spray Book

Written by Paula Mandy

Illustrated by S. K. English

One fine afternoon, in late winter,
Fairy Nurse Rhian was making her way to the reed
marsh for the starlings' Great Murmuration Display.

This year, Head Fairy had asked Rhian to tell the story of why the starlings dance. When she arrived, Rhian saw her fairy friends settled by the reeds, waiting for the evening's performance.

"Attention please, everyone," called Rhian. "As we watch this evening, I want you to remember, that it was through a great kindness to all fairies everywhere that the starlings earned their hearts."

"Really?" asked one small fairy, "Starlings have more than one heart?"
"No," said Rhian, "I mean the white hearts they wear on their feathers! Starlings did not always look as they do today. Once, they were the most glorious of birds..."

“Once, many years ago, in the days when starlings’ feathers were bright and colourful, a terrible sickness came upon the fairies.

"It would start with a tickly cough.
Later they would develop fever, become breathless and terribly weak.”

At the hospital, nursing fairies tried all they could,
but the sickness was too strong.

Affected fairies lay limply in their beds, too weak to move and every day more would fall ill.
Nursing fairies fell ill too, leaving fewer and fewer to look after the sick.

We were struggling to cope, but then I had an idea.
"We should summon the unicorn," I said.
"The unicorn has the greatest healing powers of all. She will know what to do."

"But, that's impossible," sighed Matron Fairy. "We have no way to call her.
The flower needed to call the unicorn does not bloom at this time of the year."

"If we can't call her, we will have to search for her," I said. "Even if I have to fly the length and breadth of the British Isles, I will seek her out."

And I set off on my quest.

My journey continued from autumn into winter.
I travelled many pathways, through frozen woodlands, hills and valleys.

Then, by an icy lakeside, I came across a flock of starlings looking fabulous in their gorgeous colours. I told them about the fairies and my quest to find the unicorn.

The starlings chatted amongst themselves.
"We will help you," they said.
And groups of starlings began to fly all across Britain in the search.

Eventually, the call went out that the unicorn had been spotted.

“She’s by the Fairy Glen Falls!” shouted Aster, one of the younger starlings. There was huge excitement and we set off straight away.

When we arrived, we found the unicorn in a mossy glen by a silver waterfall.
I told her about the great sickness.

“There is a way to help the fairies,” said the unicorn.
“BUT... it calls for great kindness and tremendous sacrifice.”

The unicorn turned to address the starlings.
"The only cure is for you to drop your colours on the sick fairies."

"If you are prepared to do this, you must go and dance directly above their hospital. Your colours will fall and you will become plain black birds, but the fairies will be saved."

However, many of the starlings were horrified.
"How could we give up our fine feathers?" said one.
"We would no longer be beautiful birds," said another.
Then Aster got up to speak. "Real beauty does not come from fine feathers," he said.

"Real beauty comes from inside us, from who we truly are. Could we be considered beautiful if we were too proud and selfish to help our friends? Our colours are mere decoration to us but they can save the LIVES of the fairies. I call on all of you who have kindness in your heart to rise up and fly with me to the fairies' hospital!"

The starlings cheered.
“He is right,” they said to one another, “it is the right thing to do!”
And as one they rose up into the air.

Once they reached the hospital, they flew high and swirled,
danced and dived in a display of breath-taking beauty.
As they did so, their colours fell from them like rainbow rain...

...and the fairies were cured!

The starlings were indeed now plain black birds.
However, from the next spring, an amazing thing happened.

As the starlings' chicks grew up, their black feathers developed a magical iridescence and were covered in little white hearts, as a symbol of kindness, generosity and sacrifice. Each year since, starlings have performed their beautiful Murmuration Display in memory and celebration of those who saved the fairies."

Just as Rhian finished her story, dusk fell and the dance began.
The fairies clapped and cheered as the starlings whirled and danced their magnificent aerial ballet, twisting and turning, moving as one, in the cool air above the waving reeds, set against the rich sunset colours of the evening sky.

And Nurse Rhian cheered loudest of them all.

Did you know?

Murmurations are real!
During the winter months, as twilight approaches, these marvellous spectacles really can be seen at many locations across the British Isles. Thousands of individual starlings flock together and they perform these magnificent displays.

You can sometimes see murmurations of starlings, near woodland, on reed beds, and even in city centres.
Below are some places famous for their particularly large and spectacular displays:

Avalon Marsh in Gloucestershire, Aberystwyth Pier in Ceredigion, West Hay Moor or Ham Wall in the Somerset Levels, Leighton Moss in Lancashire, Fen Drayton in Cambridgeshire, Slapton Ley in Devon, Marazion Marsh in Cornwall, Albert Bridge in Belfast, Gretna Green in Dumfriesshire and Brighton Pier in Sussex.
Can you guess which place is in this picture?

Have you ever seen a starling?

Watch out for a black bird speckled with little white hearts and sometimes, when the light catches it just right, you may even see a hint of colour in the starling's lovely, glossy plumage.

The Fairy Glen Falls, where the unicorn was found, is a real place too!
There are two Fairy Glen Falls in Britain.
One is in North Wales and the other is on the Isle of Skye.
Both are remote, beautiful and magical places.

Glossary

Aerial
Something that is aerial is in the air. In this story, the starlings' dance is described as aerial because it happens up in the air. The word is suggestive of something that is light, airy and flowing.

Iridescent
Something that is iridescent has a colourful, metallic sheen which gradually changes from your viewpoint with the light. Starlings have iridescent feathers. Peacocks have iridescence in their tails and male mallard ducks have iridescent green heads. Iridescence can also be seen in soap bubbles.

Murmuration
A murmuration is the name given to a large group of starlings as they swoop, twirl and twist, flying in unison, usually just before dusk.

Quest
A quest is a difficult, often lengthy journey which has a specific mission or goal. Nurse Rhian goes on a quest to find the unicorn.

Starling
A starling is a medium sized bird about 20cm long. Adults have glossy black plumage with green/purple iridescence speckled with little white hearts. Youngsters have some light brown feathers. Starlings are noisy and sociable birds that are normally seen in groups.

Printed in Great Britain
by Amazon